For Louisa

this book belongs to
Roseanne Marie
Keith

All Shapes and Sizes

Shirley Hughes

WALKER BOOKS
LONDON

Boxes have flat sides,
Balls are round.

High is far up in the sky,
Low is near the ground.

Some of us are rather short,
Some are tall.

Some pets are large,

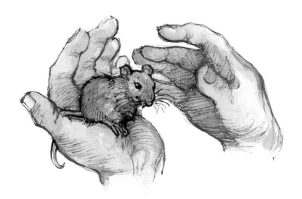

Some are small.

Our cat's very fat,
Next door's is thin.

Big Teddy's out,
Little Teddy's in.

Squeeze through narrow spaces,

Run through wide,

Climb up the ladder,

Slip down the slide.

Get behind to push,

Get in front to pull.

This jar's empty,

Now it's full.

Hats can be many sizes,

So can feet,

Children of all ages

playing in the street.

We can stand up very straight,

or we can bend.

Here's a beginning,

and this is the end!